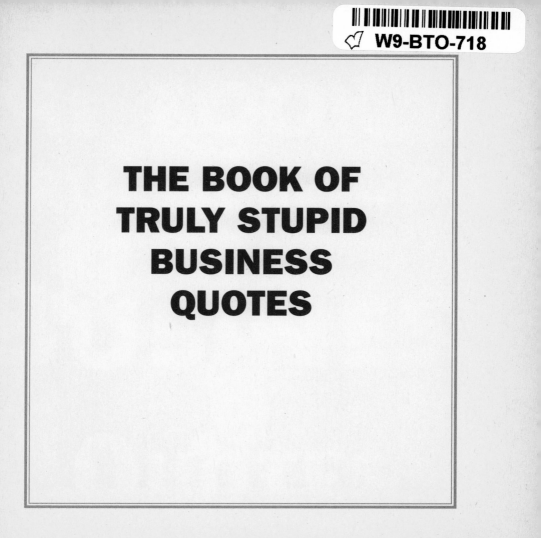

THE BOOK OF
TRULY STUPID
BUSINESS
QUOTES

THE BOOK OF TRULY STUPID BUSINESS QUOTES

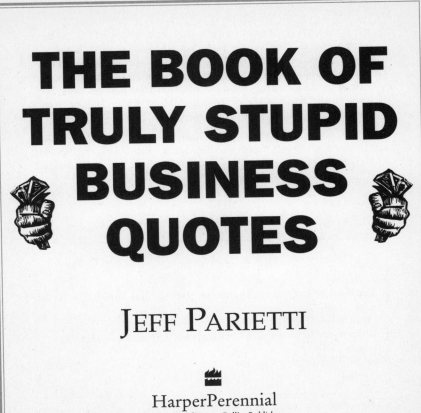

JEFF PARIETTI

HarperPerennial
A Division of HarperCollinsPublishers

HarperCollins books may be purchased for educational, business, or sales promotional use. For information, please write to: Special Markets Department, HarperCollins Publishers, Inc., 10 East 53rd Street, New York, New York 10022.

FIRST EDITION

Designed by Elina D. Nudelman

Library of Congress Cataloging-in-Publication Data

Parietti, Jeff.
    The book of truly stupid business quotes / Jeff Parietti. — 1st ed.
        p.   cm.
    ISBN 0–06–273507–1
    1. Business—Quotations, maxims, etc. 2. Business—Humor.
I. Title.
PN6084.B87P37 1997
650—dc21   97–23816
                                                                          CIP

97 98 99 00 01 ❖/HC 10 9 8 7 6 5 4 3 2 1

CONTENTS

Mouse Mortgage

PREFACE

One day during the era of our prehistoric ancestors came a moment of great importance.

The invention of the wheel? No.

The use of fire? Nah.

Why, the first business transaction, of course!

Perhaps it involved Urg trading his trusty club to Ogg to obtain a shiny stone necklace for his wife's anniversary present. (More likely was Urg's wife swapping his club for a necklace because he had forgotten to get her a gift!)

No matter. Thus commerce was born and the rest, as they say, is history!

While no scribe was around to capture the immortal words, "You've got yourself a deal!", this work offers an amusing collection of modern-day quotes from the business world. Turn to any page and you'll find a variety of funny, witty, sarcastic and just plain truly stupid remarks to enjoy.

I have included the best material selected from hundreds of quotes gathered during an intensive research process. To maintain the original essence of each quotation, company affiliations and titles are listed as of the time the individual made the comment.

Compiling this book has involved a combination of hard work and laughter. For helping me appreciate both qualities, this book is dedicated to my parents, Walt and Peggy, and my grandmother, Emily.

Also, thanks to my three brothers, one sister, two sisters-in-law, three nephews, and the rest of my many relatives, friends and coworkers for their support.

Special thanks to all the professionals on the Harper-Collins team who helped make this project come to fruition.

Finally, thanks to you, the reader. May this book offer you many hours of laughter and enjoyment!

Jeff Parietti
September 1997

Chapter 1
PERSONALITIES

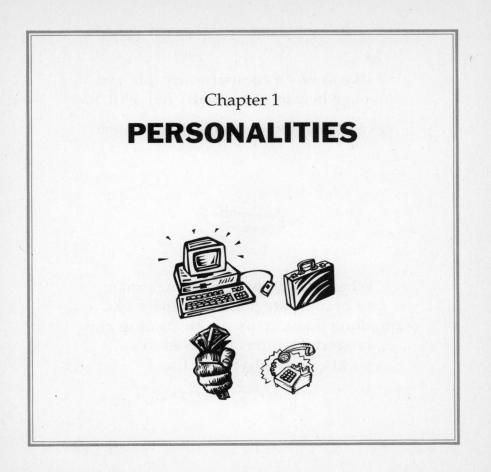

"I like to buy a company any fool can manage because eventually one will."

—Peter S. Lynch, former head of Magellan Fund at Fidelity Investments

"When you become a businessman you become stagnant in some ways. You don't do as many of the exciting and dangerous things you used to do. It was skydiving or this."

—George Steinbrenner

**"You can't be bored with greatness.
It's better to be honestly arrogant than
falsely humble."**

—"Chainsaw Al" Dunlap, turnaround artist known
for drastically cutting staff and reviving
struggling companies

**"A full moon blanks out all
the stars around it."**

—Ted Turner, on himself

"You can never bet against Michael Eisner. He's a real businessman. He can add and subtract."

—Michael Fuchs, ex-chairman of HBO and Warner Music Inc., on outlook for Walt Disney Co. under Chairman Eisner

"It should be someone incredibly handsome."

—Donald Trump, asked who should star in *The Donald Trump Story*

"Bill has tried to become more charming, but it's sort of like Dan Rather trying to be cuddlier."

—David Coursey of *P.C. Letter* on Microsoft's Bill Gates

"I go to bed happy at night knowing that hair is growing on the faces of billions of males and on women's legs around the world while I sleep. It's more fun than counting sheep."

—Warren Buffett, whose Berkshire Hathaway owns about 10 percent of The Gillette Company

"According to my mom, I'm such a big shot that she's threatening to have her uterus bronzed."

—Steven Spielberg

"I come from an environment where, if you see a snake, you kill it. At GM, if you see a snake, the first thing you do is go hire a consultant on snakes."

—H. Ross Perot

"To work here you have to be cuckoo— like me."

—UN Secretary-General Boutros Boutros-Ghali

"He's not at all odd. He's a billionaire."

—Then New York City Mayor Ed Koch on Leon Hess, Amerada Hess chairman and New York Jets owner

"It's a good thing God doesn't let you look into the future, or you might be sorely tempted to shoot yourself."

—Lee Iacocca, recalling five years later his decision to join Chrysler

Chapter 2

ENTREPRENEURSHIP

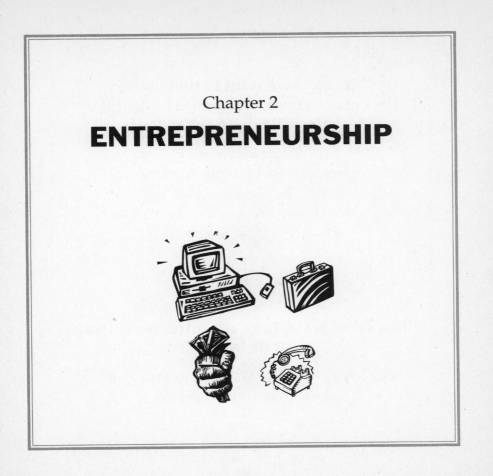

"I think if we want to understand the entrepreneur, we should look at the juvenile delinquent."

—Abraham Zaleznik,
Harvard Business School professor

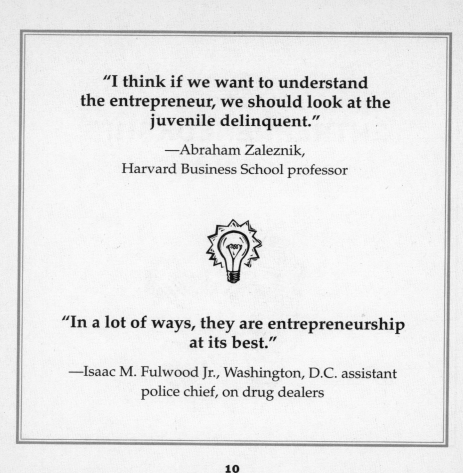

"In a lot of ways, they are entrepreneurship at its best."

—Isaac M. Fulwood Jr., Washington, D.C. assistant
police chief, on drug dealers

"If you want to make $8,000 a year standing in the rain, it's a great business."

—Bart Wilson, president of Caravali Coffees Inc., on operating a Seattle espresso cart

"This may be a new version of Junior Achievement, but you can't knock the entrepreneurial spirit."

—Donald Frizzle, Amherst, Mass. school superintendent, on student's plan to put condom machines in school bathrooms

"We say here that everybody wants to be a chicken's head, not a bull's toenail."

—Chien-Shien Wang, vice minister for economic affairs, on Taiwan's proliferation of small businesses

"It's a very big letdown. I was hoping it would flood so my business would pick up."

—Bill Ribkee, owner of Florida carpet cleaner company, on Hurricane Erin's business-costing, minimal effect

"We didn't really expect there would be a rash of sales."

—Entrepreneur Mary Lehmann of Wisconsin, on low sales of her nearly $1,000 do-it-yourself coffin

"My son is now an 'entrepreneur.' That's what you're called when you don't have a job."

—Ted Turner on his son, Ted Turner IV, who formerly worked for Turner Broadcasting Corp.

Chapter 3

GOTTA HAVE A PRODUCT

"I think I'm filling a niche no one else has touched. That of the 1 A.M. or 2 A.M. worm."

—Vend-A-Worm inventor Tom Sziszak, on machine offering cup of 25 fishing worms for a buck

"It has a strong, fruity fragrance accentuated with floral top notes."

—Mark Cash, ad manager for Exxon's British subsidiary, describing odor of new diesel fuel under testing

"It's masculine, clean and crisp with a blend of woods, particularly deep moss, to give it an outdoorsy smell and a note of bright citrus. It's a very masculine scent. It's not for quiche eaters."

—Marshall Bank, executive with jeans manufacturer Jonbil, on its unique Long Haul Cologne for truck drivers

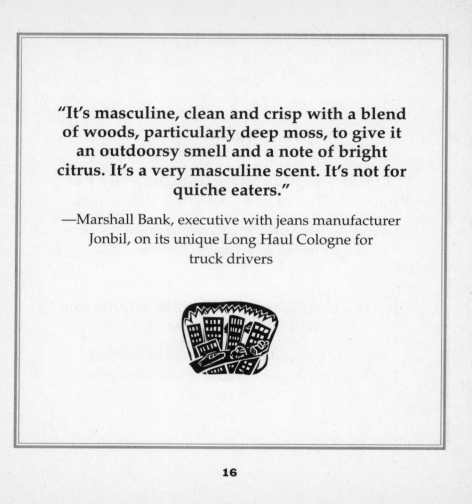

"I think that'll be a hot item for Valentine's Day."

—Sandy Quinn, marketing consultant to Richard Nixon Library, regarding facility's "Property of Richard Nixon Athletic Department" shirt

"It's a little bit like cocaine. Once you're hooked you can't live without it."

—John Rock, Oldsmobile Division general manager for GM, on the ease of a novel autonavigation system

"We also offer automatic fire extinguishers for those times when, you know, someone throws a Molotov cocktail into your car."

—Clerk Bob Schatz of a Manhattan shop peddling countersurveillance and antiterrorist equipment

"The can isn't as user-friendly as it used to be."

—Anthony Adams, director of market research, on why his Campbell Soup Co. was pursuing new can plans

"I think the attraction of our brand . . . is first of all that it is highly transparent. [Investors] can touch and see and feel the product. You don't have to be a technician to find out which advantage [the products] offer."

—CEO Fritz Humer of Viennese lingerie manufacturer Wolford AG

"Fingerprinting is a problem if you have either injured your hand or you don't have one. With this system, you can use virtually any part of your anatomy."

—Peter Puttick of Britain's Mastiff Electronics Systems, which is devising "smelly" technology to ID people by their unique smell

"We want to go after those situations where we know there is a high propensity for people to want to communicate outside of where they're staying."

—MCI's John Jacquay, on the prison pay phone product niche

"Men find new technology appealing even if they don't know what they want it for."

—Oliver Strimpel of Boston's Computer Museum, explaining why some men covet and crave latest machines

"Women prefer tabloids because their arms are shorter."

—Mort Zuckerman, *New York Daily News* publisher

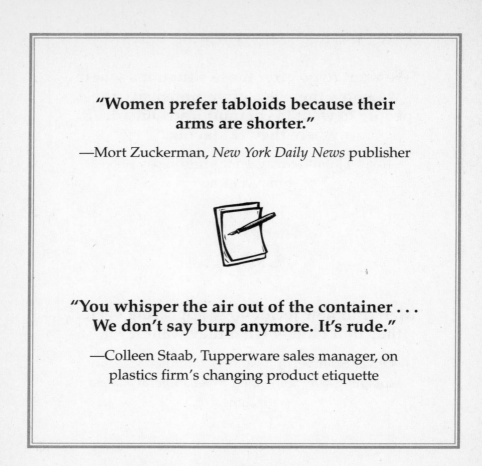

"You whisper the air out of the container . . . We don't say burp anymore. It's rude."

—Colleen Staab, Tupperware sales manager, on plastics firm's changing product etiquette

"The banana is an important product and deserves to be treated with respect and consideration."

—International Banana Association president Robert Moore, protesting to PBS about its AIDS program which employed a banana to illustrate condom use

"Maybe we should do what Mattel does: Put a sign on it that says, 'Batteries not included.'"

—E. Thomas Pappert, Chrysler Corp. sales executive, looking to produce and sell electric cars without awaiting an electric battery

"Barbie is 35 years old. Today, Mattel introduced her latest accessory—Barbie's ticking biological clock."

—Jay Leno

"The most interesting products are the ones that people need but can't articulate that they want."

—CEO Livio DeSimone of Minnesota Mining and Manufacturing

"Waste is a substance waiting for recognition."

—William Parish, former real-estate lawyer, who opened first commercial plant that burns cow manure to generate electricity

Chapter 4
THE SELLING PROCESS

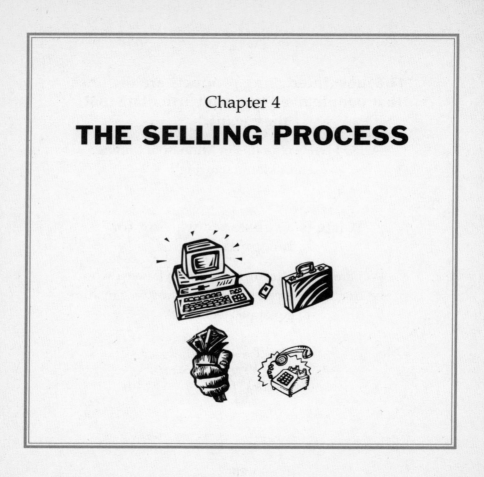

"Our motto was, 'Shameless exploitation in pursuit of the common good.'"

—Paul Newman, on his start at selling salad dressing and donating profits to charitable causes

"Early to bed, early to rise, work like hell and advertise."

—Columbia Sportswear head Gert Boyle, selected as one of America's top businesswomen

"Jim [Barksdale] is like the World War II general, you know, in the movie *Patton*. The one played by the guy in the American Express commercial."

—Craig McCaw on Netscape's Jim Barksdale, an ex-colleague at McCaw Cellular

"If he's lying, he's lying very well, which would make him an excellent PR guy."

—Matt Zachowski, president of New York public relations firm Nycom Associates, joking about Oliver North's Iran-Contra congressional testimony in 1987

"He was a strange man. He wasn't very good at marketing it."

—Christie's auctioneer Charles Allsopp on Vincent van Gogh, whose "Sunflowers" went for $39.9 million but was originally thought worthless

"It's like giving sight to the blind."

—Sim Wong Hoo, Creative Technology Ltd. chairman, pushing miracle of his firm's 3-D computer-game sound system

"Bagels are the hottest thing since sliced bread. In fact, they are sliced bread."

—Gary Gerdemann, spokesman for
Einstein Bros. Bagels

"We tried to think of something else to promote. But all we really have here are mosquitoes."

—Dana Pomerenke, Clute parks & recreation director,
on town's annual Great Texas Mosquito Festival

"If there was a market in mass-produced portable nuclear weapons, we'd market them too."

—Amstrad head Alan Sugar, considered
not the prince, but king of Britain's consumer
electronics market

"The cows are filling their bellies every day, so they might as well pay for their upkeep."

—English farmer Harry Goode, on draping his cattle
with advertising signs during mad cow disease scare

"I am certain that half of what I spend on advertising is money wasted. But I don't know which half."

—John Wannamaker, Philadelphia department store magnate

"The whole secret is low mileage. It's very Freudian. Everyone wants a virgin."

—Michael Sheehan, Costa Mesa, Calif. car dealer, explaining sales trade secrets

"It's not good with sex scandals, but in the U.S. this has helped us get out Astra's name without having to pay expensive advertising fees."

—Astra board member Lars Ramqvist, on termination of drug firm's chief exec for alleged sexual harassment

"New Yorkers are like cockroaches of the human race. They are very tough. They will happily go out shopping in this kind of weather."

—Barneys executive Simon Doonan, on New York "blizzard" shoppers

"The stores will look like a cross between an up-to-the-cabin look and a Western lifestyle look in a not-cute, real-world way."

—J'Amy Owens, head of Retail Group, describing proposed retail store connected with Robert Redford

"It's now reached the point that if you buy a toaster you get a free savings and loan."

—Lloyd Bentsen, Senate Finance Committee chairman, on S&L mess

"We're thinking of running ads that say, 'You'll just fly over our cars.'"

—Mark Muller, Suzuki Samurai dealer in St. Charles, Mo., in 1988

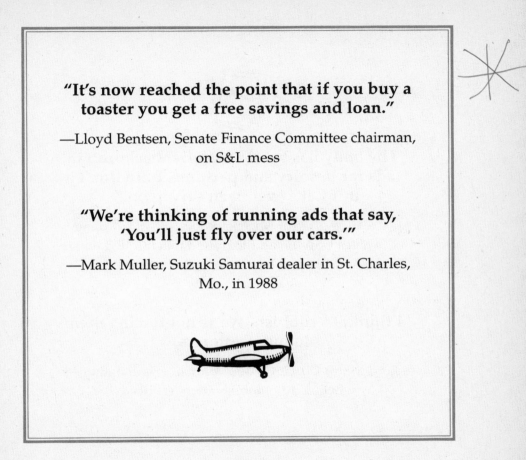

"The body has been a material backdrop in ads for jewelry and perfume, but I don't think it's ever been driven on."

—Creative director Michael Robertson of Cordiant PLC's Bates USA, on ad for Hyundai that rolled where advertising had never rolled before

"I think it's rubbish. We're not forcing them to buy Explorers."

—Ford Motor Co. CEO Alex Trotman, commenting on whether automobiles are overpriced

"Mr. Clifford could sell hams in a synagogue."

—Congressman Chalmers Wylie of Ohio, assessing Clark Clifford's 1991 testimony in BCCI bank scandal hearings on Capitol Hill

"Aeroflot Airlines: You Have Made the Right Choice."

—Ad campaign theme for only airline in then Soviet Union

"I've got to say I know little or nothing about the advertising business."

—Edsel B. Ford II, upon becoming advertising manager for the Ford Division of Ford Motor Co.

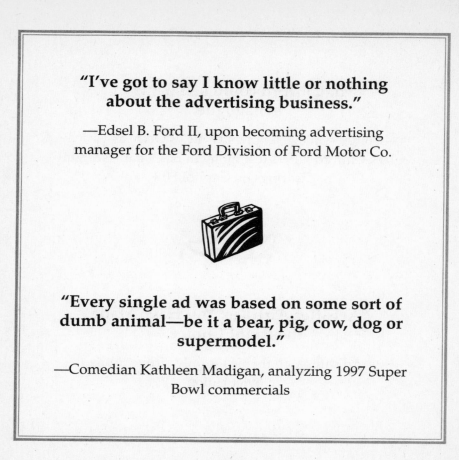

"Every single ad was based on some sort of dumb animal—be it a bear, pig, cow, dog or supermodel."

—Comedian Kathleen Madigan, analyzing 1997 Super Bowl commercials

"If walls could talk, that would be good."

—Realtor Mike Tarantino, upon listing the house where President Bill Clinton resided during law school

"She'll very likely blimp up again."

—Marvin Sloves, chairman of Louce and Partners/SMS ad agency, on his thumbs down advice against using Duchess of York Sarah Ferguson in Weight Watchers ads

"You shouldn't ask for the cheapest, you should ask for the least expensive. This is Republican stuff, and they don't use the word cheap."

—Grover Price, asked about "cheapest" item in his Washington, D.C. souvenir stand during George Bush's presidential inauguration

"You can buy a machine gun, explosives, pornographic books and movies, and go to topless clubs in Ohio, but you can't buy Bad Frog Beer."

—Jim Wauldron, Bad Frog Brewery Co. president, on Ohio's refusal to permit sales of the product which features a frog making an obscene gesture

"Some of the advertising would make a used-car dealer blush."

—Warren Burger, then Supreme Court Chief Justice, on the introduction of lawyer ads

41

Chapter 5

IT'S A ZOO OUT THERE

"Over a long weekend, I could teach my dog to be an investment banker."

—Herbert Allen, president of investment banking firm Allen & Co. Inc.

"What am I supposed to haul my dogs around in, a Rolls-Royce?"

—Wal-Mart's Sam Walton, on why he drove a pickup truck

"The heifers are 20 percent smarter since they started reading it."

—Duane Ashbeck, Wisconsin dairy farmer, whose cows get shredded newspapers for bedding instead of straw

"We're located on the eastern edge of a migratory path for ducks, geese and pigeons. . . . The day a rabbit can jump 400 feet in the air, we'll get more serious about them."

—Joel Genty, environmental supervisor at Charles de Gaulle Airport in Paris, on the 50,000 rabbits living between runways

"If you drop a dead cat off a tall enough building, he's going to bounce."

—Binkley Shorts, manager of Over-The-Counter Securities Fund, on resiliency of small stocks that were beaten down

"The market's stronger than goat's breath."

—Mike Hiley, Smith Barney Inc. oil trader, after crude oil prices pushed to an eight-month high

"If you can pick women, you can pick cattle. You look for good angularity, nice legs and capacity."

—Bobby Hull, NHL Hall of Fame member and cattle rancher

"Buffaloes are better looking than cows. They don't have fat all over their butts."

—Ted Turner, on why buffaloes were in and cows were out on his Montana ranch

"There are a lot of sacred cows in Wyoming, and cows are one of them."

—Pete Williams, spokesman for Congressman Dick Cheney of Wyoming, on prominence of ranching in the western state

"It's pretty much a tortoise pace. But at least the tortoise is moving more quickly, maybe like an aardvark or something."

—Congressman Charles E. Schumer of New York, on movement toward Tokyo stock exchange allowing in foreign firms

"The crew will consist of one pilot and a dog. The pilot will be there to nurture and feed the dog. The dog will be there to bite the pilot if he touches anything."

—Earl Wiener, management science professor at University of Miami, discussing 21st-century aircraft before Air Line Pilots Association

"We're sure a dog as wise and loving as Tige is not a pit bull."

—CEO Kent C. Robinson of Buster Brown Apparel, on firm's trademark dog

"I think a lot of us could hear the tiny patter of mouse feet in the halls."

—Anonymous CBS employee, on why some thought Walt Disney Co. might begin a friendly takeover bid for the network

"They won't stick their heads in the sand but they will stick their head through a fence and forget how they got it there."

—Ostrich expert Leslie Sutherland of Anderin Ostrich Farm Inc. in Monroe, Wash.

"When it comes to the information highway, we're roadkill."

—Gilbert F. Casellas, head of Equal Employment Opportunity Commission, lamenting his division's lack of computerization

Chapter 6
THE COMPETITION

"I really believe our ultimate competitive advantage is the fact we essentially went broke."

—CEO Thomas Theobald of Continental Bank, formerly Continental Illinois

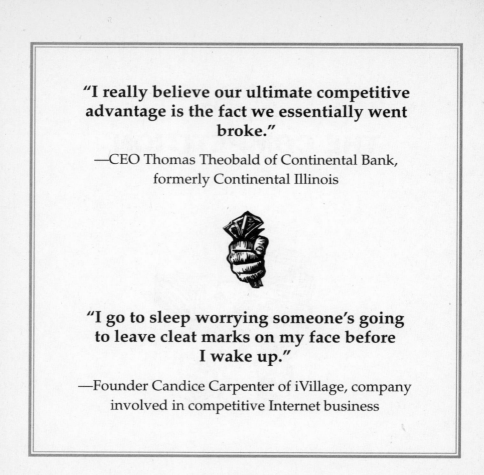

"I go to sleep worrying someone's going to leave cleat marks on my face before I wake up."

—Founder Candice Carpenter of iVillage, company involved in competitive Internet business

"In 1992, Germans used 170 million condoms, Britons used 160 million. The French used 100 million. We can catch up, but we must go faster."

—Philippe Douste-Blazy, France's health minister

"We're more of an adult-driven pickle and are not into babyish humor."

—Claussen pickles brand manager Tim Cofer, comparing its ads with those of rival Vlasic pickles

"Espionage is probably too strong a word when you're talking about masked peas."

—Steven Poole, Gerber Products Co. spokesman, asked if factory tours were halted due to fear of corporate spies

"We haven't got any interest in Mr. Kendall's nose."

—Coca-Cola president Donald R. Keough, asked if entry into Soviet market in 1985 was to tweak nose of Chairman Donald M. Kendall of PepsiCo, which got there first

"There isn't a big line [of competitors] forming. It's not a particularly attractive vocation."

—Mike Gallagher of R.O.S. Head Service, which collects waste from boat toilets at Everett (Wash.) Marina

"Competition is a way of life. If you don't have a really tough competitor, you ought to invent one."

—Quaker Oats CEO Bill Smithburg

"I couldn't believe no one had addressed the mule market."

—Sharon Doherty, Vellus Products president, on discovering a market niche for mule shampoo and conditioners

"If Ed McMahon dies or is arrested on a morals charge, American Family Publishers will be in a bad way."

—David Sayer, Publishers Clearing House spokesman, on why firm doesn't use celebrities in advertising

"In the takeover business, if you want a friend, you buy a dog."

—Carl Icahn

"We have no competitors. We bought most of the competitors."

—CEO Gordon Eubanks Jr. of Symantec Corp., which produces computer network software

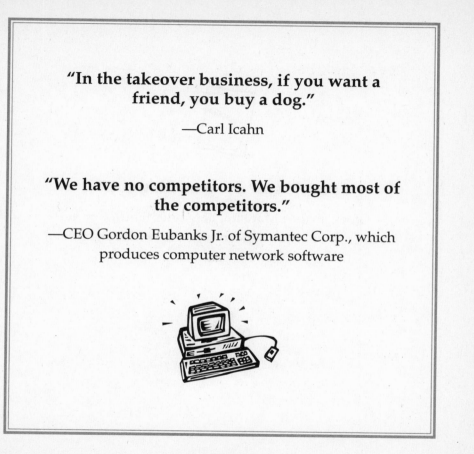

"People still use pencils, right?"

—Stock analyst Marc Regberg after Smith Corona Corp., one of last American typewriter manufacturers, filed for bankruptcy

Chapter 7
NAME CALLING

"I find it rather easy to portray a businessman. Being bland, rather cruel and incompetent comes naturally to me."

—British actor John Cleese, who portrays executives in commercials and training films

**"Other people are schmucks.
I am not a schmuck."**

—Donald Trump, asserting that he got out of the stock market before Crash of '87

"If all the economists were laid end to end, they would not reach a conclusion."

—George Bernard Shaw

"The three C's explain it all. Their members are either comatose, co-opted, or corrupt."

—Joseph Grundfest, retiring commissioner at the Securities & Exchange Commission, on why corporate audit committees fail

"Bo takes over with the complete confidence of everyone at the paper. And it is good to have a president whose first name can be the tiebreaker in area spelling bees."

—Donald Graham, Washington Post Co. chairman, naming Boisfeuillet Jones Jr. as *Washington Post* president and general manager

"It was the Americans that did virtually all the selling today. They're such a bunch of loonies."

—Antoine Massabni, trader at SBS Valeurs in Paris, analyzing drop in financial stocks on Paris exchange

"Asking your average consumer to evaluate a name like Navistar or Unisys is like asking an Eskimo to evaluate artificial snow."

—Jeanette Lerman, Unisys executive, on report that customers were more likely to recognize renamed firms by old names

"I'm not even sure what the term 'CIO' means. I've only been one for 15 years."

—Ken Fielding, Omaha Public Power Department
chief information officer

"Harley [Davidson] is maybe the best brand name in the U.S. Coca-Cola is a good brand name, but people don't tattoo it on their bodies."

—Ralph Wanger, Chicago mutual fund manager

"My father always told me that all businessmen are sons of bitches, but I never believed it until now."

—President John F. Kennedy on 1962 showdown with U.S. Steel over price hikes

"It was mostly the nerds, weirdos, and outcasts who built this industry. None of us had anything to do on a Friday night."

—Vern Raburn, who opened a computer store in Los Angeles way back in 1976

"The reason we are called domestic car dealers is that all the rich people out here buy our cars for their domestics because their kids won't drive them."

—Leonard Ely, Chevrolet dealer in Menlo Park, Calif.

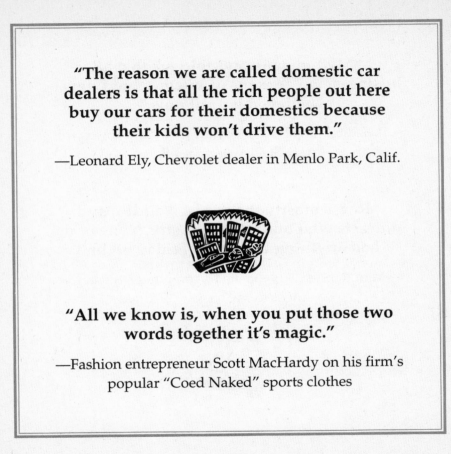

"All we know is, when you put those two words together it's magic."

—Fashion entrepreneur Scott MacHardy on his firm's popular "Coed Naked" sports clothes

"What do you call someone who doesn't know about operating systems and doesn't want to? Normal."

—Scott Cook, Intuit executive

"The difference between Texaco's reputation and Hugh Liedtke's reputation is the difference between chicken manure and chicken salad."

—Attorney Joe Jamail, representing Pennzoil and its chairman Liedtke, on a $14 billion lawsuit which claimed that Texaco induced Getty Oil to break its deal to sell out to Pennzoil

"That means we're going to have to read another terrible book."

—U.S. Rep. Barney Frank of Massachusetts, pondering possible impact of $300,000 fine for ethics violations against sometime author Newt Gingrich

"I've been laboring here for five years and now we have a sock talking at our commencement."

—Recent Southampton College of Long Island grad Samantha Chie, on her college's move to give an honorary degree to Kermit the Frog

"Most professors of finance can't hold an intelligent conversation with a vice president of finance."

—Prof. Noel Tichy of the University of Michigan

"The United States has got some of the dumbest people in the world. I want you to know that. We know that."

—Ted Turner, speaking to an international forum examining the direction of U.S. society

"He's nuts. He's been nuts for years, and I'd like to ask what he's ever done for this country."

—J. Peter Grace, chairman of W.R. Grace, on Ralph Nader

"I think he's a pig. He has his snout in the trough almost 24 hours a day, and you can quote me."

—Graef Crystal, executive pay consultant, on putting Leonard Tow of Citizens Utilities Inc. on his list of 10 most overpaid CEOs

Chapter 8
DEADLY DEALINGS

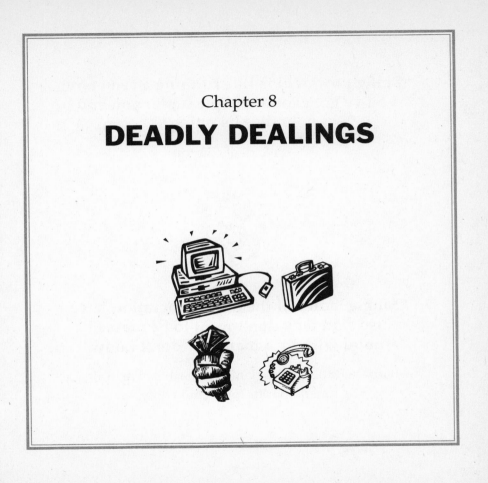

"Being president is like running a cemetery; you've got a lot of people under you and nobody's listening."

—President Clinton

"Single ladies of the older generation have also said they don't want to be messed around with by a man they don't know."

—Barbara Butler on England's "Martha's Funerals," a funeral parlor for women only

"Income from operations was 23 percent stronger this quarter than in the third quarter of last year. These operational results are especially gratifying in light of the continuing unfavorable trends in the mortality rate."

—Chief executive R. L. Waltrip of SCI, a leader in the funeral and cemetery business

"No matter how statistically cheap the stock is, when you think that euthanasia for management should be the corporate strategy, you really shouldn't own it."

—Marc Perkins of Perkins Capital Advisers

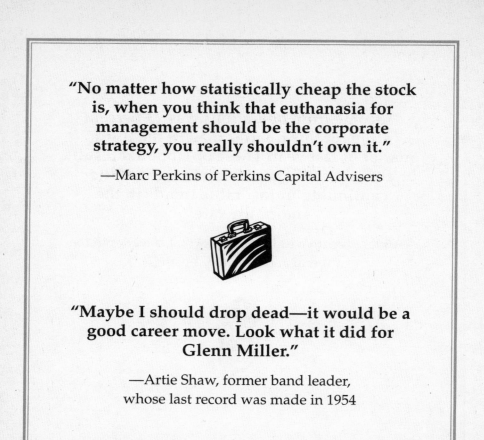

"Maybe I should drop dead—it would be a good career move. Look what it did for Glenn Miller."

—Artie Shaw, former band leader, whose last record was made in 1954

"I think grandpa would look a heck of a lot better in a box made by the grandchildren than in one from a factory in Ohio."

—Undertaker Al Carpenter, touting his firm's $9.95 assembly instructions booklet for build-it-yourself coffins

"They're most comfortable working with the dead."

—James Spears, Federal Trade Commission general counsel, on recent college graduates' attraction to trust and estate work

"Sure, it's going to kill a lot of people, but they may be dying of something else anyway."

—Othal Brand, Texas pesticide regulatory board member, on termite killer Chlordane

"If people here were not getting killed on the job in homicides, we would have quite a low rate of fatalities."

—Samuel Ehrenhalt, Labor Department official, on statistics which showed murder to be the leading cause of work-related deaths in the Big Apple

"The trick is to make sure you don't die before prosperity comes."

—Chrysler chairman Lee Iacocca on
bright sales forecasts

Chapter 9

MANAGEMENT MUSINGS

"It takes geniuses to build businesses and idiots to ruin them."

—Joseph Brooks, CEO of women's fashion chain
Ann Taylor

"There are natural seeps all over this country. Oil in the water is a phenomenon that has gone on for eons."

—Exxon exec Don Cornett, trying to downplay impact
of 1989 major oil spill before Alaskan fishermen

"The stupidity of brilliant people never ceases to amaze me."

—Jeno Paulucci, CEO of Luigino's Foods

"One of the stupidest things I ever did was call everybody owners."

—Ex-chairman Robert Iverson, a force behind forming an employee-owned Kiwi Air Lines, but later axed by employee-run board

"I must admit that my management style was too simple sometimes."

—Chinese track coach Ma Junren, confirming that his methods sometimes included hitting members of world-class team

"A bunch of guys take off their ties and coats, go into a motel room for three days, and put a bunch of friggin' words on a piece of paper— and then go back to business as usual."

—General Manager John Rock, GM Oldsmobile Division, on company mission statements

"I believe the new trends include the requirement on the part of the customer that the vehicle will work."

—Chairman Sir Graham Day of Rover Group, a British automaker, on customer expectations

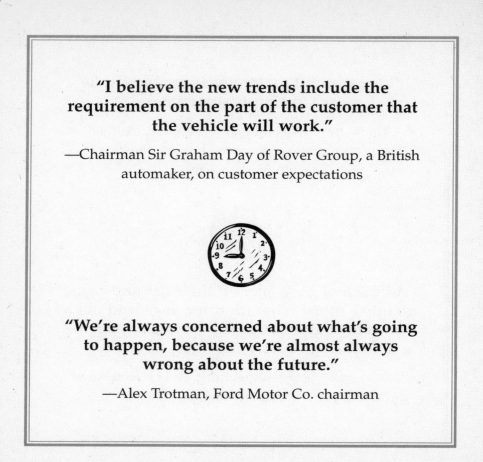

"We're always concerned about what's going to happen, because we're almost always wrong about the future."

—Alex Trotman, Ford Motor Co. chairman

"Well, I really don't know because I don't believe in doctors. But number one, I feel fine. Number two, I swim a mile every day. And number three, I'm single, so I get laid all the time."

—Peter Benjamin Lewis, Progressive Corp. CEO, queried on his health status by a possible investor

"Corporately, we believe in orgasms."

—Warren Littlefield, NBC Entertainment president, regarding female chat about sexual fulfillment on debut of NBC TV drama "Sisters"

"We figured out that a customer base with a salary was better than a customer base with an allowance."

—President Michael A. Weiss of Express, a group of profitable women's clothing stores associated with The Limited

"My worst board was five people strong, and two of them had to be brought in on stretchers. One was 87 and one was 83. They just laid them on a table in the back of the room, and that's how they got their quorum."

—Douglas Austin, Toledo financial services consultant

"Strategies are okayed in boardrooms that even a child would say are bound to fail. The problem is there is never a child in the boardroom."

—Victor H. Palmieri, turnaround artist

"It takes five years to develop a new car in this country. Heck, we won World War II in four years."

—H. Ross Perot

**"If it makes money, we expand it.
If it doesn't, we cut its throat. . . "**

—Poultry czar Don Tyson, senior chairman of
Tyson Foods

**"Once you've made the philosophical
decision not to commit suicide, you're
committed to being an optimist."**

—Roberto Goizueta, Coca-Cola CEO

"Life is like a bicycle. Whoever stops pedaling will fall over."

—Sabastiao Ferraz de Camrgo Penteado, on why he was still active at 80 as head of Brazil's largest construction firm

"We used to be so inbred it's a wonder we didn't have an eye in the middle of our foreheads."

—Bill Salter, Sears executive vice president, on bringing in management talent from outside to turn around the company

"Bureaucracy grows faster than anything, and it doesn't even need water."

—Lord Gordon White of Hanson Industries

"The job of all good chief executives is to destroy good ideas."

—Reuters CEO Peter Job

Chapter 10
SUCCESS & FAILURE

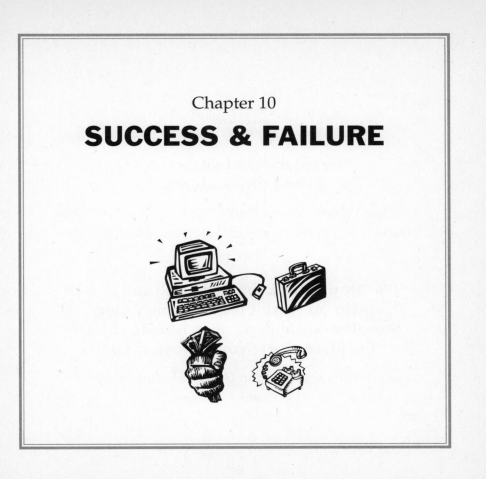

**"I used to own two airplanes.
Now I own a bicycle."**

—Clive Francis, former British land baron, quantifying
impact on him of Lloyd's of London financial troubles

**"It's OK to have a company fail, and to start
again. At least it is in Silicon Valley.
Sometimes you don't even have to change
the place where you park your car."**

—Venture capitalist John Doerr of Kleiner, Perkins,
Caulfield and Byers

"It wasn't easy. I had to work at it."

—Oilman John J. "Mad Jack" Stanley, on how he
managed to "hit" bankruptcy twice in 10 years

**"After 150 years, we've finally
learned how to run a railroad."**

—CEO John W. Snow of CSX, summing up company's
nearly 20 percent increase in quarterly profit despite
flat revenues

"One thing that bodes well for it is that we're not hampered by any recent success."

—John Rock, general manager of
GM's Oldsmobile Division

"Our goal is world domination, just like Microsoft."

—Naveen Jain, InfoSpace Corp. CEO and ex-Microsoft
employee, on his Internet-related startup company

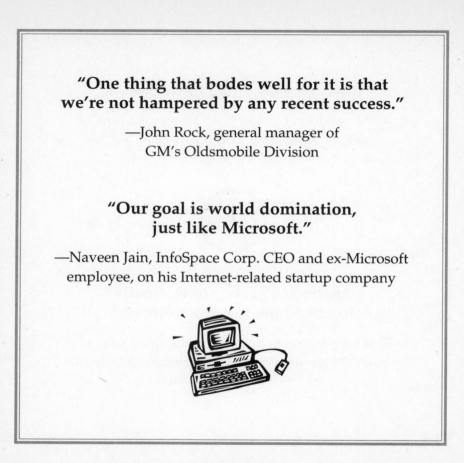

"It's not a failure. What we're doing is just delaying another success."

—Commander Frank Culbertson Jr. of space shuttle *Discovery*, after fourth launch delay came seconds before liftoff

"I never thought I'd see the day I would be bragging about potentially losing 'only' a billion dollars, but I guess that day has arrived."

—U.S. Postmaster General Anthony Frank, after somewhat succeeding by reducing size of Postal Service's annual deficit

"Losing money has had a wonderfully clarifying effect."

—CEO William Van Fassen of Blue Cross and Blue Shield, on company's likely $40 million loss and his 25 percent pay cut

"All you have to do to run a cable [TV] company is get a license from the city and be mean to your customers."

—Ralph Wanger, mutual fund manager

"The market has been decimated. The esthetic augmentation business has gone flat."

—Donald Stepita, former president of National Capital Society of Plastic Surgeons, on shrinking breast-implant sales due to health concerns

"We're buying the most expensive programming available and taking it off the air quickly."

—CEO Robert Wright of National Broadcasting Co., explaining network TV

"When you take a blue-chip company and turn it into a buffalo-chip company, that's not a good situation."

—Robert A. Brusca, chief economist of Nikko Securities International, disapproving of corporations willing to assume enormous debt for takeovers and LBOs

"It was the luck of the Irish."

—Toy store manager Les Morris on how John Gotti Jr., son of so-called crime family godfather, was able to find and buy case of popular Tickle Me Elmo dolls during the holidays

"Obviously, he won't be paying for the parking."

—Shawn Good, vice president of Silver Cloud Valet Northwest, after a customer's car was accidentally lost for seven weeks at Sea-Tac International Airport

"It is better to be approximately right than precisely wrong."

—Warren Buffet

"Macy's has promised not to let us build in any place that is going to have an earthquake."

—Caravali Coffees president Bart Wilson, on plans to expand into California department stores

"We hope Mr. Liddy's infamy will work in reverse."

—Thomas E. Ferraro, president of new security firm founded by Watergate figure G. Gordon Liddy, on strategy for attracting business

"Sometimes there's a certain genius in ignoring the facts."

—Robert Wussler, Turner Broadcasting senior exec, on Ted Turner's success in businesses thought to be unpromising

Chapter 11
THE FEDERAL SCENE

"We know this looks like it might be complicated."

—IRS official Arthur Altman, explaining a new "simplified" tax form in 1986

"It's just that we wanted it to arrive as soon as possible."

—A U.S. Postal Service spokesman, after letters stating that postal service was better than ever were sent via courier to the Federal Trade Commission

"What next, do we cut checks to companies that remember to lock their doors at night?"

—U.S. Rep. Dick Armey of Texas, on large food companies receiving $9 million in advertising funds through an Agriculture Department program

"We did what we did, and we didn't do what we didn't do."

—Paul A. Volcker, then Federal Reserve Board chairman, explaining action to support the dollar

**"I guess I should warn you, if I turn out t[o]
particularly clear, you've probably
misunderstood what I've said."**

—Fed chairman Alan Greenspan

**"His answer, as usual, was very unclear.
. . . He used Greenspan language . . . "**

—Yoh Kurosawa, Industrial Bank of Japan president,
on Fed chairman's comment about a possible interest
rate rise

"I still can't make any sense out of Fed Chairman Alan Greenspan's pronouncements."

—Robert E. Lucas Jr., University of Chicago professor, after winning 1995 Nobel Prize for economics

"I am guardedly optimistic about the next world but remain cognizant of the downside risk."

—New York economist Jeremy Gluck, proposing words for Alan Greenspan's tombstone

"Recalling a cigarette because it contains a smelly chemical is like recalling the Titanic because there are splinters in the railing."

—Executive director John Banzhaf of "Action on Smoking and Health," after filters tainted with an irritating chemical resulted in a tobacco firm having to recall eight million cigarettes

"It proved that I had a heart, which surprised a lot of people."

—Former Treasury Secretary William E. Simon, on his heart surgery

"I know my mail is delivered on time. I assume everyone else's is also."

—Loews Corp. president Preston Robert Tisch, on his appointment as Postmaster General

"Averages don't always reveal the most telling realities. You know, Shaquille O'Neal and I have an average height of six feet."

—Four-foot-ten Labor Secretary Robert Reich

Chapter 12

STOCKS & INVESTMENTS

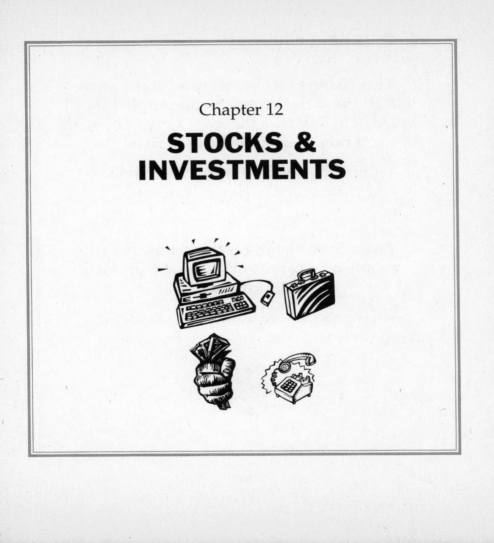

"This fishing tackle manufacturer I knew had all these flashy green and purple lures. I asked, 'Do fish take these?' 'Charlie,' he said, 'I don't sell these lures to fish.'"

—Charles T. Munger, Berkshire Hathaway vice chairman, on investor misjudgments

"As a Stasi agent, I learned how to sell people on a cause—it's a good skill for a stockbroker."

—Guenter Schachtschneider, former East German secret policeman, on his new profession

"The recommendations I am about to give you are fundamental recommendations. As for more speculative recommendations, we'd like to give you those over the phone."

—Bank analyst Matthew Czepliewicz, Credit Suisse First Boston in London, during breakfast for potential investors

"I think they'll be able to sell the stocks. For one reason or another, there are plenty of men around who would like to own shares in a whorehouse."

—Perrin Long of Lipper Analytical Securities, sizing up IPO of Nevada's Mustang Ranch

"I was an inexperienced investor."

—Robert Citron, Orange County, Calif. treasurer for more than 20 years, after his investment strategy allegedly pushed county into bankruptcy

"Had I been managing money in 1972, I would have been in growth stocks. And I'd probably be driving a taxi today."

—David Schafer, manager of Schafer Value Fund

"They are investing in management-challenged companies. How's that for politically correct?"

—William Benedetto, chairman of Benedetto, Gartland & Greene, on Kohlberg, Kravis Roberts & Co.'s focus on financially struggling firms

"$1,000 left to earn interest at 8 percent a year will grow to $43 quadrillion in 400 years, but the first 100 years are the hardest."

—Sidney Homer, Salomon Brothers analyst

"Owning Euro Disney shares is like riding Space Mountain: You go up and down but you're always in the dark."

—Fund manager Steven Schaefer of London's Oeschle International Advisers

"I've known people to spend more time comparison shopping for paper towels than for investments."

—SEC chairman Arthur Levitt

"There are two times in a man's life when he should not speculate: When he can't afford it and when he can."

—Mark Twain

"I'm putting my money where my mouth is."

—Warren Buffet, avid Cherry Coke drinker, on buying more than $1 billion in Coca-Cola stock

"For the *Wall Street Journal* to criticize my wife for making money is like *Field and Stream* criticizing someone for catching a fish."

—President Bill Clinton, regarding Hillary Clinton's $98,000 profit on a $1,000 commodities investment

"Let the buyer beware. There is nothing like the sizzle of Ollie North to make a deal soar, but then again, a sizzling steak can be nothing more than an old dead cow."

—*IPO Aftermarket* newsletter publisher John Fitzgibbon, after stock price of Guardian Technologies International Inc.—headed by North—more than doubled on its first day of trading

"It's a great site. Where else do you find 72 acres of land just ripe for development?"

—Real-estate developer Sam Tuchman, after receiving regulatory go-ahead to build housing tract near Love Canal

"The atmosphere there is not conducive to holding Tupperware parties."

—Investor relations head Christine Hanneman of Premark International Inc., explaining a possible quarterly earnings drop from Japan operations after Kobe earthquake

"All I am is a professional opportunist."

—Major real-estate investor Samuel Zell, who has a reputation for buying low and selling high

"You have to understand reinsurance before you go into it. And then you really shouldn't go into it."

—Beneficial Corp. CEO Finn M. W. Caspersen, on moving to sell the company's reinsurance unit

"Every Wall Street cowboy and his brother is thinking about catching this big move."

—Consultant Anthony Collins of Staley Commodities International Inc., regarding hog futures rise in anticipation of a report expected to show pork production cuts

Chapter 13
INSIGHTFUL ANALYSIS?

"Recession is when you tighten your belt. Depression is when you have no belt to tighten. When you have lost your trousers, you are in the airline business."

—Adam Thompson, ex-chairman of British Caledonian Airways Ltd.

"We have lots of buyers and not a lot of sellers, and that makes for higher prices."

—Dudley Peel, equity trading managing director for Donaldson Lufkin & Jenrette Securities, with startling insight into a Dow rise

"What's going wrong is that the economy is doing better than anyone expected it to do."

—Chief economist Fred Levin of
Eastbridge Capital Inc.

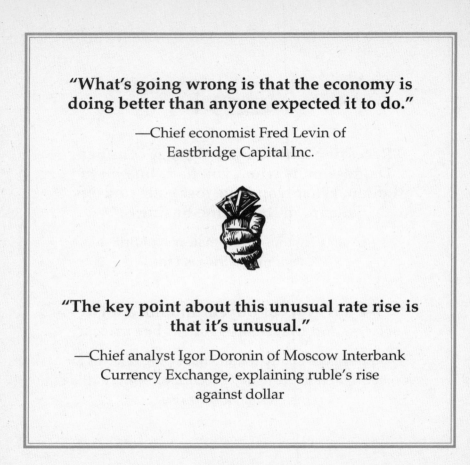

"The key point about this unusual rate rise is that it's unusual."

—Chief analyst Igor Doronin of Moscow Interbank
Currency Exchange, explaining ruble's rise
against dollar

"It's such a very small percent of total users that would be impacted in any way as to be nonimpactful."

—Executive Casey Hughes of computer distributor Merisel, analyzing effects of Intel's Pentium chip crisis in 1995

"I am cautiously pessimistic."

—Andrew Card, head of American Automobile Manufacturers Association, on chances that Japan would open its auto market to foreigners

"You can't tell who's swimming naked until after the tide goes out."

—David Darst, Goldman Sachs vice president, on futility of trying to predict which LBOs would survive a recession

"We're like the Starship *Enterprise*. We are going where no man has gone before."

—Nike marketing executive Andy Mooney, on firm's $175 athletic shoe

**"Hey, if you can't take people's money
and then screw 'em,
then you've got no business
being in the business."**

—San Francisco Mayor Willie Brown, on authorizing
city's lawsuit against tobacco firms despite their
contributions to his election campaign

**"IBM is a dinosaur that Lou Gerstner is
putting on an exercise program and a diet.
So you have a leaner dinosaur,
but it's still going extinct."**

—Neal Goldsmith, Tribeca Research Inc. president,
commenting in late 1993 on cost-cutting moves
by IBM's CEO

"I think we're on the road to coming up with answers that I don't think any of us in total feel we have the answers to."

—Mayor Kim Anderson of Naples, Fla. on city's management troubles

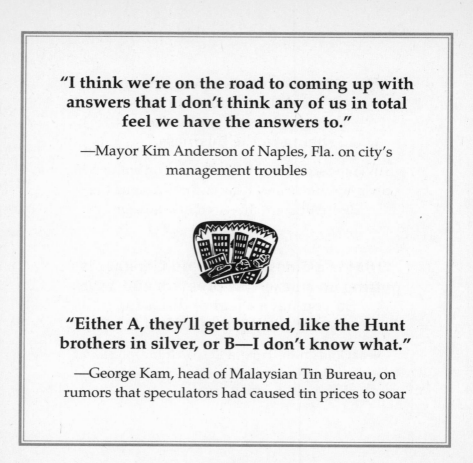

"Either A, they'll get burned, like the Hunt brothers in silver, or B—I don't know what."

—George Kam, head of Malaysian Tin Bureau, on rumors that speculators had caused tin prices to soar

"You give people half fare and they'll get on the damn plane if they see a wing hanging off."

—Union leader Don Owen, on how Eastern Air Lines was still flying despite machinists' two-year strike

Chapter 14
RELIGIOUS FERVOR

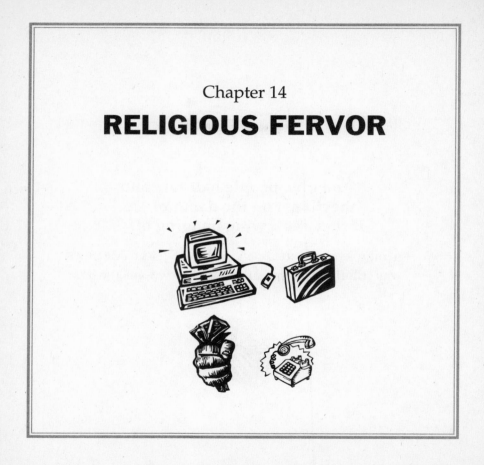

"I'd say, 'It's a Buttmaster, Your Holiness.'"

—Suzanne Somers, on how she would answer if
the Pope asked the name of the exercise machine
she promotes

**"Thank God I started the company, because
otherwise I couldn't get a job here."**

—Signature Eyewear CEO Bernard Weiss,
on workplace high-tech changes

"It is important that monks have work to do."

—Father Tryphon, All-Merciful Saviour Russian Orthodox Monastery, on move to peddle such gourmet coffee blends as Abbot's Choice and Byzantium

"The meek shall inherit the world, but they'll never increase market share."

—William G. McGowan, MCI Communications chairman, after rapidly expanding firm okayed two-for-one stock split in early 1980s

"It's where dealers tell us God intended the horn to be."

—Louis E. Lataif, Ford Division general manager, explaining why Ford Motor Co. decided to switch horn from turn-signal lever to steering wheel on many 1984 models

"Tact is the ability to tell a man to go to hell and get him excited about going there."

—Auctioneer Jerry King of Fletcher, N.C.

"To insist on a complete definition of what is right and what is wrong would be going too far."

—Claude Rosenberg, president of RCM Capital Management, on whether guidelines were required to prevent sometimes irresponsible, dishonest presentations by money managers

"We've been searching for you, God!"

—American Family Publishers sweepstakes notice— generated by computer—received by Florida's Bushnell Assembly of God Church

"*Eternity* magazine will cease publishing with the January issue."

—Item from a news service focusing on religion

"Our ambition is not business, but to love God. To love God, one must live. To live, one must balance one's budget."

—Abbot Dom Sebastian of monastery Notre Dame des Dombes, on his monks making and selling a high protein food used by mountain climbers

"It's nothing but a Christian Disneyland, a 'Six Flags over Jesus.'"

—Protestor Bob Eckhardt, on Jim Bakker's
Heritage USA

"When cows have to choose between God's time and government time, they will give milk on God's time."

—U.S. Rep. Thomas Tauke of Iowa, voicing opposition
to proposed daylight savings time extension which
eventually passed

Chapter 15
WORKIN' FOR A LIVING

"Basically, I try to be as charming and ingratiating as I can without making myself vomit."

—NBC's Katie Couric, discussing how she gets the story

"Not every cow is photogenic."

—Cow photographer Kathy DeBruin, on why a cow's hide must be combed, brushed and spray-painted before a photo shoot

"Every morning I get up and look through the *Forbes* list of the richest people in America. If I'm not there, I go to work."

—Robert Orben, former speechwriter for
President Gerald Ford

"I don't have too much work. Once you're 90, people don't tie you up for long-term projects."

—Architect Philip Johnson, 89, after accepting job to
design a cathedral

"After finding no qualified candidates for the position of principal, the school department is extremely pleased to announce the appointment of David Steele to the position."

—Philip Streifer, Barrington, R.I. schools superintendent

"I was supposed to be director of engineering, but there were so few of us that they made me director of operations. My first assignment was to get a post office box so we could get literature describing the equipment we couldn't afford to buy."

—Andy Grove, Intel CEO

"I looked at it as a way to go to the ballpark every day and not be considered a bum."

—Oakland Athletics CEO Wally Haas, citing one reason he initially took a job with the team

"It's a nice break from working on my inaugural address."

—Bob Dole, on why he agreed to do a television ad for credit card company after losing the 1996 presidential election

"Yes, the king of the deadbeat dads is now the Avon lady."

—Jeffrey Nichols, once jailed for failing to pay more than $600,000 in child support, on his new job of selling beauty products

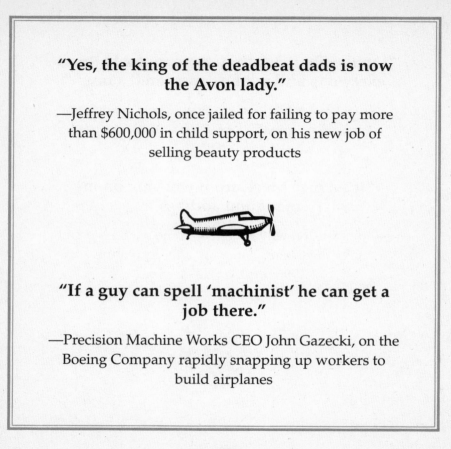

"If a guy can spell 'machinist' he can get a job there."

—Precision Machine Works CEO John Gazecki, on the Boeing Company rapidly snapping up workers to build airplanes

"I'm tired of hearing about money, money, money, money, money. I just want to play the game, drink Pepsi and wear Reebok."

—Shaquille O'Neal, upon inking a $121 million contract with the Los Angeles Lakers

"I sort of thought I wanted to be an anthropologist. But my father suggested I go to a cocktail party full of anthropologists first. I did. He's a very wise man."

—Actress Tea Leoni

"What they do for a living is not our concern. It's whether the project has good community outcomes."

—Kerry Mumford of Australia's national arts agency, on group's move to help fund training video for prostitutes

"[He] was just doing his job."

—Spokeswoman Shelley Clark for New York City's Tavern on the Green, on doorman who unwittingly called cab for two thieves

Chapter 16

SHOW ME THE MONEY

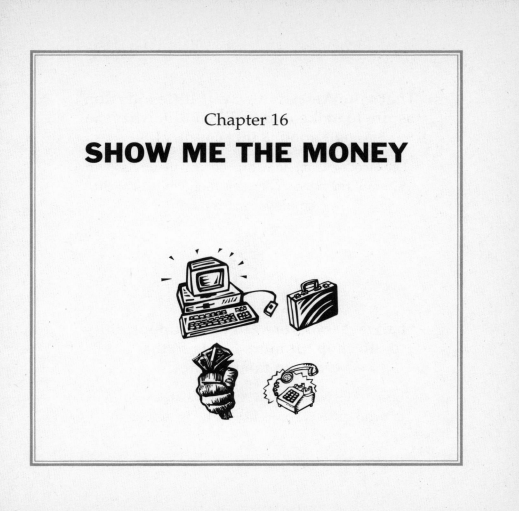

"That's the American way. If little kids don't aspire to make money like I did, what the hell good is this country?"

—Lee Iacocca, Chrysler Corp. chairman, on receiving $20 million in total compensation while firm cut employee merit pay

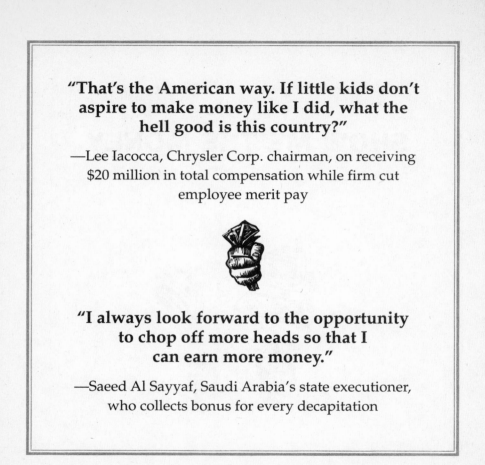

"I always look forward to the opportunity to chop off more heads so that I can earn more money."

—Saeed Al Sayyaf, Saudi Arabia's state executioner, who collects bonus for every decapitation

"It costs a lot of money for us to make our places look cheap."

—CEO Jim Sinegal of Price Costco,
a major warehouse discount chain

"I still have trouble paying 75 cents for a Snickers."

—Multimillionaire John Edward Anderson,
Ace Beverage founder

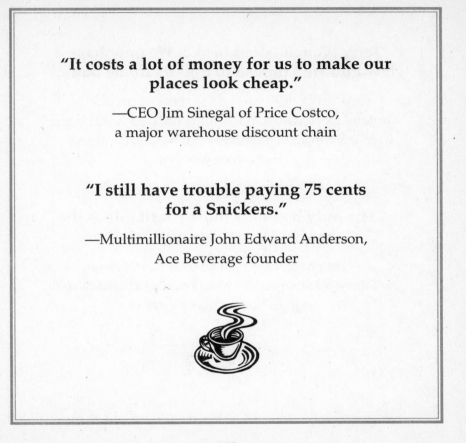

"Jerry [Garcia] died broke. We only have a few hundred thousand dollars in the bank."

—Deborah Koons Garcia, wife of the late
Grateful Dead leader, after judge ordered her to honor
$5 million settlement between her husband and
his ex-wife Carolyn

"The only business more profitable is the mafia. Or maybe software."

—Hambrecht & Quist analyst Kurt Kruger,
on Johnson & Johnson's Palmaz-Schatz coronary stent
used to unclog major arteries

"We just want good people to run for office. And if you want that, you gotta pay for it."

—Alan "Ace" Greenberg, former Bear Stearns CEO, on company contributing $169,000 to reelection campaign of New York Gov. Mario Cuomo

"About 10 years ago, the insurance companies discovered that they didn't have all the money in the world and they wanted the rest of it."

—Pharmacy owner Joe Tuley, on how independent pharmacists' profits have been squeezed by insurers

"I may have made a bazillion dollars this year, but the corporation got the money."

—Fitness guru Susan Powter,
who had to file for personal bankruptcy,
on her Susan Powter Corporation

**"One number is as good as another.
When you get that high, what difference
does it make?"**

—James Squires, spokesman for presidential candidate
Ross Perot, asked whether Perot's net worth was $2.2
billion or $3.3 billion

"We wanted to do something to enhance our guests' ski experience during the busiest periods . . . so we decided to raise ticket prices during the 13 busiest days of the year."

—Wayne D. Hoss, president of Mount Mansfield Co., which owns a ski resort in Stowe, Vermont

"Cheer up, son. To my ears, that is the sound of profit."

—McDonnell Douglas CEO Harry Stonecipher to onlooker, as one of the firm's jet fighters made a loud takeoff at Farnborough International Air Show

Chapter 17

EMPLOYEES & OFFICE AFFAIRS

**"We needed the single-mindedness
of people who think about chocolate
24 hours a day."**

—Nestle CEO Helmut Maucher

**"There are workaholics who spend most of
the night in these boardrooms. You see who's
bleeping whom, and I don't mean just in the
corporate sense."**

—Trump Tower resident Charlotte Ozawa,
on mischief in nearby office buildings

"If people would only behave themselves, the prices of tires would go down."

—Goodyear CEO Robert Mercer, explaining in 1988 that rubber condom and glove demand due to AIDS had increased tire raw-material costs

"We converse with a lot more people via the Internet, only to discover that most of them are talkative idiots, just like at the office."

—Orson Scott Card, science fiction author

"If you empower dummies,
you get bad decisions faster."

—Harley-Davidson CEO Rich Teerlink

"Employers who automate but take people
out of the process are lobotomizing their
factories. A human is the cheapest, totally
flexible and reprogrammable machine
money can buy."

—Manufacturing consultant Tom Blunt

**"This is not a layoff,
this is operations improvement."**

—Peggy Slasman, Massachusetts General Hospital
spokeswoman, on cutting more than 400 employees

"They can't fire you if they can't find you."

—Former CBS correspondent Charles Kuralt, joking
about real motives behind doing *On the Road* series

"They're going to have a lousy Christmas anyway."

—Management consultant Lester Tobias,
on companies' laying off workers during the holidays

"Biological solutions are the most cost-effective. You don't have to pay bugs a big salary."

—Biotech company CEO Louis Fernandez of Celgene,
about using new "bio-bug" technology to clean up
hazardous wastes

"Product development was like elephant intercourse. It was accompanied by much hooting, hollering, and throwing of dirt, and then nothing would happen for a year."

—Brunswick CEO Jack Reichert

"We deliver about 1.5 million e-mails per day; and most people in this company feel like they're getting all 1.5 million."

—Bob Walker, Hewlett-Packard Co.
chief information officer

"We have a saying around Bank of America. Kill the messenger only if he's late with the news."

—Ron Rhody, director of corporate communications

"Saying Patrick Buchanan speaks for workers is like saying the Ayatollah Khomeini speaks for priests and rabbis."

—AFL-CIO President John Sweeney

**"It's a weird picket line.
Writers are out there holding up signs and
there's nothing on them."**

—Johnny Carson, during a 1988 writers' strike of his
NBC show

**"We pull them in and work them to death.
And then they begin moving in sushi circles
and lose touch with Velveeta and the people
who eat it."**

—Gordon S. Bowen, Ogilvy and Mather
executive creative director, on how new ad execs
eventually lose touch with their mainstream audience

"Like everybody else at ITT, I spent a lot of time on airplanes. I'm not sure what we were doing, but we were doing it in a hurry."

—PepsiCo chairman D. Wayne Calloway,
on working for ITT's Harold Geneen in the 1960s

"The generation that was once associated with dropping acid in order to escape reality is now dropping antacid in order to cope."

—James W. Hughes, Rutgers University professor
of urban planning, regarding baby boomer
money pressures

Chapter 18

DRESS FOR SUCCESS

"Our dress code is, you must dress."

—Sun Microsystems CEO Scott McNealy on
company's relaxed office attire

**"It's a historic moment for the company and
for athletic supporters in general."**

—Bike Athletic Co. spokesman Randy Black, marking
manufacture of firm's 300-millionth jockstrap

**"In bras, ladies and gentlemen,
you find gold."**

—Pierre-Alain Berend, organizer of inaugural
European lingerie conference

**"I will be in Omaha or New York as the
circumstances require. My mother has sewn
my name in my underwear, so it'll be okay."**

—Warren Buffet, on holding down two jobs at once—
Berkshire Hathaway chairman and Salomon Inc.
interim chairman

"We're the only one with the royal warrant in corsetry. Quite honestly, it is a great honor because mine is as personal a royal appointment can get."

—June S. Kenton, codirector of Rigby & Peller corsetiere—by Queen of England's appointment

"Designer jeans are nice, but a lot of people feel they can cover their rear ends without going broke in the process."

—Kurt Barnard of Barnard's Retail Marketing Report, on a $211 million IPO by Guess Inc.

"A lot of players are starting to wear more athletic briefs these days to allow more movement, or, should I say, less movement."

—Michael Jordan,
on a new underwear line he helped design

"You ought to see this new line of cheese underwear."

—Jean Swain, Milwaukee store manager,
on fast-selling Green Bay Packer "Cheesehead" wares
leading up to the team's latest Super Bowl victory

"This is without precedence in men's fashion history. It's reflective of a growing objectification of the male body in our culture."

—Clothes expert Richard Martin, Metropolitan Museum of Arts' Costume Institute, on introduction of men's underwear with derriere padding

"If the men want to take off their jackets, feel free to. And, if the girls want to take off their blouses, it's all right with me."

—Ted Turner, before the National Press Club

Chapter 19
THE BOSS

"Who am I, the Queen?"

—"King of Software" Bill Gates, replying to administrative assistant's request to hire help to handle his growing influx of calls and letters

"I can tolerate one or two mistakes, then I'll cut their hearts out with a spoon."

—CEO Katherine Hammer, Evolutionary Technologies International, about her scientists

"Well, he does have a very dynamic zero-defect program."

—Lt. General Thomas Kelly, on Saddam Hussein reportedly "eliminating" Iraq's top Air Force commander because of insubordination during Gulf War

"In all fairness, there were others who didn't get along with him. He's a very difficult man to work for."

—FBI agent Anthony Nelson, discussing case in which employee put cyanide in boss's water cooler

"Anybody incapable of punching me in the face is probably incapable of being a group executive for Grand Met."

—Allen Sheppard, boss of Britain's
Grand Metropolitan conglomerate

"I believe in what I'm doing. The fact the chairman gets out there and talks about his own products, and makes a fool of himself occasionally helps."

—Chairman Richard Branson of Britain's Virgin Group

"Things were run on a need-to-know basis: if you needed to know, you weren't told."

—Former Maxwell publishing empire exec Peter Jay, on late boss Robert Maxwell

"One of the reasons I was so delighted to talk to you today is that the alternative was to go to work."

—Citicorp Chairman John S. Reed during a speech to an industry group

"I'm having the most fun I've ever had in business. I never had a company come to me before and say, 'How fast can you spend money?'"

—CEO Richard A. Snell of Tenneco Automotive

"If he starts telling me what to do, I am going to spank him and send him to bed without his dinner."

—Veteran editor Paige Rense of *Architectural Digest* on her new, relatively young Conde Nast boss— James Truman, 35, who succeeded octogenarian Alexander Liberman

**"Rupert's got a pretty good eye.
If you're good, you get to live.
If you're bad, you don't."**

—CEO Roger Ailes, Fox News Channel,
on Rupert Murdoch

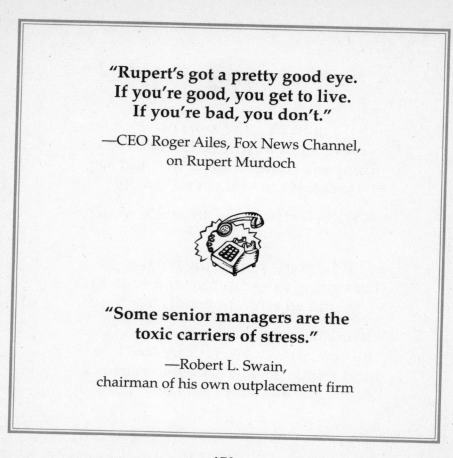

**"Some senior managers are the
toxic carriers of stress."**

—Robert L. Swain,
chairman of his own outplacement firm

Chapter 20
NEPOTISM

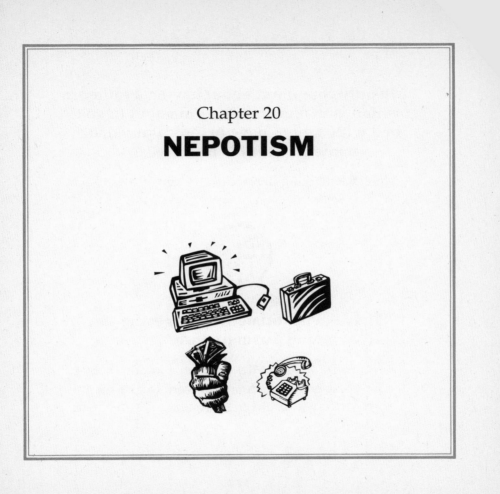

"My only complaint about having a father in fashion is that every time I'm about to go to bed with a guy I have to look at my dad's name all over his underwear."

—Marci Klein, daughter of fashion king, Calvin Klein

"I have to negotiate with her every day and I usually lose."

—U.S. Trade Rep. Mickey Kantor, joking that Japanese government might want to hire his 10-year-old daughter

"So many people have claimed to be the father of the Mustang that I wouldn't want to be seen in public with the mother."

—Lee Iacocca, on receiving credit
for the Ford Mustang's success

"I want a blood test."

—Ex-Treasury Secretary Donald T. Regan,
on implications that he helped "father"
savings and loan crisis

**"The rich daddy is dead.
We're the wicked stepmother."**

—Osicom Technologies CEO Sharon Chandha,
promising cost-cutting after buying Rockwell's
unprofitable network systems division

**"I made my money the right way. My
grandfather gave it to me."**

—Rep. Joseph P. Kennedy (D-Mass.), joking at
Michigan fund-raiser

**"I never dreamed when I married a
Rockefeller that I would wind up spending
half my time asking people for money."**

—Sharon Percy Rockefeller, president of
Washington, D.C. public television station,
on fund-raising obligations

**"Why would Cinderella want to
marry a butcher just because he's got a few
yen in his pocket?"**

—David Wu, S.G. Warburg & Co. analyst, minimizing
rumors of an Apple Computer and Canon Inc. merger

**"She asked for a fashion magazine,
and I went out and got her *Vogue*."**

—Publisher Samuel Newhouse who bought
magazine publisher Conde Nast, and its holdings,
as wife's anniversary present in 1959

**"The perfect fund manager is a guy who
can't pick his kids out in a police lineup."**

—Michael Stolper, investment consultant

"Almost everything I have is for sale, except my kids and possibly my wife."

—Carl Icahn, on his move to sell stock back to Saxon Industries following a class-action suit

"It's like watching your mother-in-law go over the side of a cliff in your favorite car. It's a case of mixed emotions."

—Leonard Green, partner in LBO firm Gibbons Green van Amerongen, on 1987 stock market crash

"CNN is the grandfather of this business—
and they have a lot of grandfathers
watching them."

—CEO Roger Ailes of Fox News Channel

Chapter 21

CAFETERIA FARE

**"Cow ears are easy to chew,
they're thin and they're very, very tasty."**

—Novapet CEO Juan Ricatti, extolling benefits of
company's top product—for dogs

**"I guess for a high-fashion restaurant
like this, the prices are okay."**

—Zhang Wei, Chinese college student, during opening
of Beijing's first McDonald's restaurant

"I wanted to open a restaurant with an affordable exotic animal. Then I was walking home one night and a rat ran across in front of me and gave me this idea."

—China's Zhang Guoxun, whose popular
Jialu Restaurant in Guangzhou includes
Lemon Deep-Fried Rat and Rat Kebab

"It's healthy for people to be in contact with a wilderness where something can eat them."

—CEO Philippe Kahn of Borland International

"We only sell right wings."

—Bob Stumpf, Cleveland meat store owner, summing up his chicken selection to Republican presidential candidate Pat Buchanan

"This is made possible by salad dressing and by the people who buy the damn stuff."

—Actor Paul Newman, on donating his firm's profits to construct a camp for critically ill children

"'Baby Bells' is sort of like 'Jumbo Shrimp.'"

—William McGowan, MCI Communications chairman
and founder, on the seven regional Bell operating
companies

**"If you run an all-you-can-eat restaurant, the
last thing in the world you want is a busload
of fat people pulling into your parking lot."**

—David Rocker, investment group president,
on Internet gridlock resulting from offers of $19.95
unlimited monthly access

"Our pizza delivery business is very dependent on cars."

—Tom Monaghan, Domino's Pizza owner, explaining why he spent $8.1 million for classic 1931 Bugatti automobile

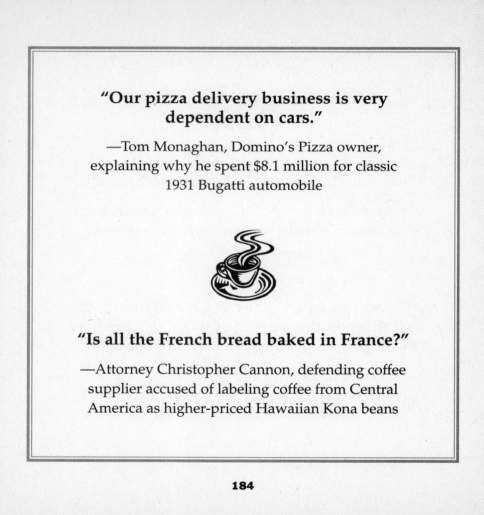

"Is all the French bread baked in France?"

—Attorney Christopher Cannon, defending coffee supplier accused of labeling coffee from Central America as higher-priced Hawaiian Kona beans

"Never eat spinach just before going on the air."

—Dan Rather, on lessons learned as
CBS Evening News anchorman

**"Americans did not fight and win wars
of the 20th century to make the world safe
for green vegetables."**

—U.S. Budget Director Richard G. Darman, discussing
merits of economic versus environmental good

"We can't feed the world on beefsteak. So noodles will conquer the world."

—Nestle CEO Helmut Maucher

"It doesn't take a lot to become a rabbit producer. You put two rabbits in a cage and that's it."

—Business development exec Douglas Doerfler of Pel-Freez, one of America's leading rabbit processors

Chapter 22

TOURISM & RETIREMENT

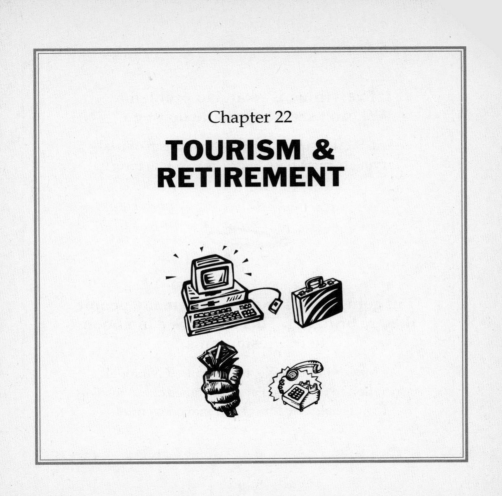

**"Everything is okay. No problems.
We can't see why people don't go."**

—Ali S. Al-Gammoudi, Libyan tourism official,
trying to push his country as vacation resort

**"I'm going to call and see how many people
they're bringing. This could be a big boon
to our restaurants."**

—Mayor Jim Naugle, on word that National
Association to Advance Fat Acceptance chose his Fort
Lauderdale city for its national convention

"We've already had a million Germans and a million British guests, and to have those numbers in France without a war going on is really something."

—Walt Disney Co. CEO Michael Eisner, assessing Euro Disney attendance

"Recognizing the great equity we had with the ape, it seemed logical to bring him back with his family to relate to the family vacation traveler."

—David Koontz, American Touristers' marketing vice president, on why firm resurrected its 'gorilla-attacking-suitcase ad' of early 1980s

"I have the pleasure now of watching daytime television. The country's really in trouble . . . but I can always call Dionne Warwick on the 'Psychic Friends Network.'"

—Retired General Colin Powell, on how he was spending some of his free time

"A lot of its readers are of an age where they forget to cancel."

—Ad executive Jerry Della Femina, assessing why *Reader's Digest* with its many retired subscribers is among magazine circulation leaders

"I wanted to look forward to a year made up of four seasons rather than four quarters."

—John J. Cullinane, on why he retired
from Cullinet Software

"It's like Mickey and Minnie have been kicked out of Disney World."

—Charlotte, N.C. waitress Sherri Thurber,
on Jim and Tammy Bakker's forced "retirement"
from their PTL empire

**"Big ideas are so hard to recognize,
so fragile, so easy to kill. Don't forget that,
all of you who don't have them."**

—John Elliott Jr., chairman of Ogilvy & Mather
International, announcing his retirement
from the ad agency

Chapter 23

INTERNATIONAL
REPORT

**"Just-in-time is the reason everyone is late.
The streets are filled with trucks making
just-in-time deliveries."**

—Shiro Fujita, president of NTT Data,
a major Japanese networking firm

"Everyone should have an Italian afterlife."

—Retired Procter & Gamble CEO Edwin Artzt,
on his job as executive director of G&R Barilla,
Italy's largest pasta-maker

**"They carry a gun like we carry a wallet.
It adds to the charm of the place."**

—Oil executive E. Anthony Copp on life in Yemen

**"It took six years, but the city of Hutchinson
finally brought the Soviet Union to its
knees."**

—Barry Anderson, Hutchinson, Minn. city attorney,
ending ban on Russian vodka sales after
Soviet Union's fall

"In Switzerland we are not known because we don't do much business here, and in the U.K. or U.S., where we do a lot of business, we are not known because we are Swiss."

—Sergio Mantegazza, CEO of Globus Travel and Cosmos Tourama

"We were definitely underweighted in Finnish potato stocks."

—Ralph Wanger, president of Wanger Asset Management, on buying 300,000 shares in Finnish food products firm

"The Prime Minister has never liked owning car companies. She barely puts up with owning the police."

—Sir John Egan on British government's privatizing of Jaguar and Rover Group—of which he is chairman

"Being naked with a bunch of guys in a sauna and being beaten with a bunch of beech leaves is not for me. But that's part of the Russian way of doing business."

—Steven Traylor, exec with an international investment group, on Russians' popular place for business meetings

"The opening quarter of the year demonstrated graphically how free trade works. We traded $20 billion in loans to Mexico and got their ex-president for free."

—Business columnist Alan Abelson

"The government has done nothing, and we're all relieved."

—Laurence Pih, president of Brazilian firm Moinho Pacifico, recalling price freezes and other failed policies that had worsened country's raging inflation

"We follow the International Monetary Fund's guidelines for Argentina."

—Milwaukee Mayor John O. Norquist
on his fiscal policies

"For some international banks, their sleaze factor is higher than their interest rates."

—U.S. Customs Commissioner William Van Raab, after indictment of Bank of Credit and Commerce International S.A. for drug money laundering

"I can't stand the proliferation of paperwork.
It's useless to fight the forms. You've got to
kill the people producing them."

—Vladimir Kabaidze, general director of Ivanovo
Machine Building Works near Moscow

"The Kuwati, he does not like to work.
The foreigners have experience that we lack,
and they work for lower salaries.
This does not mean that the Kuwati
does not contribute. But this way,
the Kuwati can stay safe and rested."

—Kalah al-Rashidi, 23-year-old Kuwati, explaining his
country's work ethic and reliance on foreign workers

"The European boat has to learn how to sail with the German elephant aboard."

—Gianni Agnelli, head of Italy's Fiat group,
on Germany's economic might

**"There has been no exclusion.
We have simply excluded all the women."**

—Nicolas Romanoff, descendant of the last Czar,
explaining dearth of female representation at meeting
to form family foundation to foster democracy
in Russia

"We have to be competitive in Europe and signal that we are a high-technology country—not just chocolate, cows, cheese and Swatches."

—Hanspecter Lengg, telecommunications exec for Migros cooperative, on Switzerland's market status

Chapter 24
ODDS & ENDS

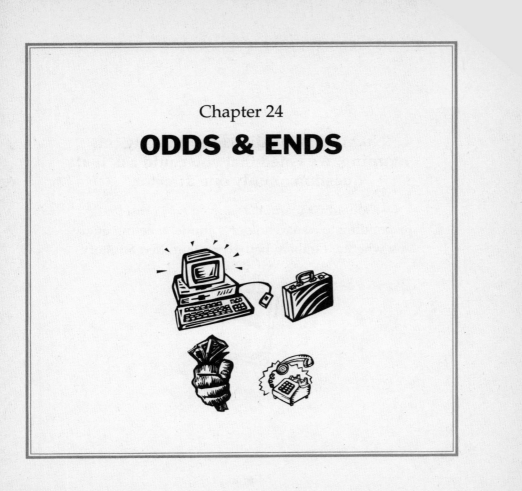

"No. And at the directors' meeting this morning, we voted that you could ask that question of only one director."

—Donald Graham, *Washington Post* president, responding to a shareholder's annual meeting query on whether Graham had ever committed adultery

"When I was a graduate student at Harvard I learned about showers and central heating. Ten years later I learned about breakfast meetings. These are America's three great contributions to civilization."

—Mervyn A. King,
London School of Economics professor

**"You know, my pappy told me never
to bet my bladder against a brewery or
get into an argument with people
who buy ink by the barrel."**

—AFL-CIO president Lane Kirkland, asked for his
opinion on media coverage of unions and labor

**"I'm not pissin' in a bottle
of no corporate cop."**

—Popular business management consultant Tom
Peters on workplace drug testing

"He *is* Mr. Whipple, and always will be
Mr. Whipple, and certainly we want to make
sure that nothing but Charmin
goes in his bathroom."

—Spokesman Mark Leaf of Procter and Gamble,
after company inadvertently stopped lifetime toilet
paper supply to actor Dick "Mr. Whipple" Wilson,
who played role for 25 years

"Before you see the credit-card industry voluntarily reduce interest rates, you will see William [The Refrigerator] Perry dancing the lead in *Swan Lake*."

—Congressman Frank Annunzio of Illinois

"He's good at dealing with people. He's not a typical computer nerd. He's well-dressed. And he bathes a lot."

—Elizabeth Horn, girlfriend of Netscape
Communications' Marc Andreesen,
after technology company's initial
public offering made him worth $50 million

**"The Internet is a solution
looking for a problem."**

—Bill Towler, founder of an Oklahoma City
computer services firm

"What the world needs is a home computer that does windows."

—Esther Dyson, computer industry newsletter publisher, commenting in the mid-eighties on the challenge of making home computers useful

"After thousands of years of dumb objects and dumb environment, now everything is going to have intelligence. Someday you may have a serious discussion with your lawn furniture. You may say, 'Why are you out here in the rain? Why didn't you go inside as I told you to?'"

—Robot show curator Robert Malone, telling schoolchildren about the future of robotics at the American Craft Museum

"Maybe it's a little understated."

—Saul Steinberg, corporate takeover expert, about his birthday party which included exotic birds, tapestry tablecloths and nude models posing as paintings

"There's nothing more therapeutic than having these bankers spend a few thousand days in jail."

—Henry A. Berliner Jr., president of Second National Federal Savings in Annapolis, Md., on punishing those who drive S&Ls into insolvency

"Money is not an issue when you believe in what you're doing."

—New York hairdresser Roger Thompson, on lost sales at his new Dallas salon from failed attempts to convince women to ditch the big blond hair look